One-Minute
PRAYERS®
to Start
Your Day

Hope Lyda

HARVEST HOUSE PUBLISHERS
EUGENE, OREGON

Cover by Bryce Williamson

Front cover image © aleksandarvelasevic / iStockphoto

ONE-MINUTE PRAYERS is a registered trademark of The Hawkins Children's LLC. Harvest House Publishers, Inc., is the exclusive licensee of the federally registered trademark ONE-MINUTE PRAYERS.

ONE-MINUTE PRAYERS® TO START YOUR DAY
Copyright © 2019 Hope Lyda
Published by Harvest House Publishers
Eugene, Oregon 97408
www.harvesthousepublishers.com

ISBN 978-0-7369-7377-9 (Milano Softone™)
ISBN 978-0-7369-7378-6 (eBook)

Library of Congress Cataloging-in-Publication Data is on file at the Library of Congress, Washington, DC.

Printed in China

19 20 21 22 23 24 25 26 / RDS-SK / 10 9 8 7 6 5 4 3 2

Contents

Beginnings

Facing the Day

*At daybreak, Jesus went out to a solitary place.
The people were looking for him and when they
came to where he was, they tried to keep him
from leaving them. But he said, "I must preach
the good news of the kingdom of God to the other
towns also, because that is why I was sent."*

LUKE 4:42-43

God, as I face a new day, help me be mindful of what you have planned. May my focus be stayed on your desires so that I do not give my time, myself, and my day to other paths or work. Grant me discernment so I can recognize when a distraction is truly an indication of your leading and not something to avoid.

It is not easy to turn my life over...even to you. But knowing there is a purpose for me up ahead, just minutes from now and as my day unfolds, I am excited to see what today might bring.

Inviting Wisdom In

The fear of the LORD is the beginning of wisdom,
and knowledge of the Holy One is understanding.

PROVERBS 9:10

I like to act like I know what I am doing most of the time, even when I am clueless. But Lord, this can get me into trouble. I pray that you would help me to seek your wisdom and leading in more circumstances. May I begin with your wisdom before stepping forth into this day and onto the path of my life.

My desire to know and understand my world and the people and situations in it will only be realized when I know you intimately.

A Day's Birth

I rise before dawn and cry for help; I have
put my hope in your word. My eyes stay
open through the watches of the night,
that I may meditate on your promises.

PSALM 119;147-148

The hope I have in you is the beginning of my possibilities, my dreams, my future. Today is the beginning of the rest of my calendar of days. May I face all that you have for me with an openness.

I wonder who will be placed in my path. Will I find an open door where I least expect it? Will one step forward today be the start of something great and of your hand?

I meditate on your promises, Lord. They fill my heart and mind throughout the night. Now, let me put my faith in those promises as a new day is born.

Giver of Life

From birth I have relied on you; you brought me forth from my mother's womb. I will ever praise you.

PSALM 71:6

When I could not yet form words that made sense to those around me...when I was unable to feed myself, walk, or consider the consequences of my actions...you were my source of care and protection. You brought me into this world, and now you bring me through this life. I praise you for today. I even thank you for the trials I face. When I am misunderstood at home or at work, or I find I have made a faulty choice, I know you are here for me.

You are the one who was with me at my beginning and will be the one to embrace me at the end of my days. Thank you for your presence and comfort every day in between.

TRUST

Trusting Your Wisdom

You will understand what is right and just and fair—every good path. For wisdom will enter your heart, and knowledge will be pleasant to your soul.

PROVERBS 2:9-10

I've always had a heart for justice. It pains me to see how people aren't treated fairly and in honorable ways. Yet I know I'm often focused on me and what serves my best interests. Redirect my mind today so that I understand what is right and just. Lord, show me where and how I'm not fair in my actions or thoughts. Do I treat some strangers online better than I treat my family? Are there people I approach with fear or trepidation rather than trust and acceptance? I want to have your eyes for everyone. I want to do what is right by you and your beloved children.

When I am hard on those I love or judgmental with people I encounter, show me what it is in my own spirit that is being challenged. Let your wisdom permeate my heart so I trust your knowledge and love to rule my character.

Doing Good

*Trust in the LORD and do good; dwell in the land
and enjoy safe pasture. Take delight in the LORD,
and he will give you the desires of your heart.*

PSALM 37:3-4

Lord, I have felt the gentle nudge of conviction lately. You have shown me how I still hold on to certain parts of my life with a tight grip that indicates more fear than trust. God, help me to serve your children and embrace my purpose from a place of security and trust. The impact of my days could be so much more if I freely lived out the desires of my heart, never withholding my time, gifts, and kindnesses.

Restore to me an unhindered longing to give to the people I love and the people you bring into my days. I want to see where the desires you place on my heart lead when I clear the obstacles of ego, fear, and doubt. I know it will be great. I trust in you to do good, even through a flawed vessel like me.

Following the True God

Blessed is the one who trusts in the LORD,
who does not look to the proud, to
those who turn aside to false gods.

PSALM 40:4

Financial worries can keep me up at night. You watched me toss and turn at all hours last night, Lord. This morning, I feel the weariness that comes when woes turn into anxiety. My prayers of faith seem to digress into mental rounds of reconfiguring the monthly bills. Pride draws me back to this place of disappointment. I thought I would be beyond this kind of worry by now.

When I realize how much energy I've given over to the small god of worry instead of to you, the God of wonder and promises, I'm eager to make a change. You remind me that I am never alone on this journey. Release me from my limited view. Fix my eyes on you and you alone and let my thoughts this morning be prayers of gratitude—so that at midnight tonight, my spirit will be resting in the rhythm of praise.

Sharing My Fears

When I am afraid, I put my trust in you. In God, whose word I praise—in God I trust and am not afraid. What can mere mortals do to me?

PSALM 56:3-4

As a child, I never liked to show my fear. Even now, I hold back from sharing my true concerns because I don't want to upset my family and friends. Lord, I feel you drawing near to me today. You embrace me and tell me to share what makes me afraid.

You reassure my anxious heart and turn fear into fearlessness. The deepest dark is dispelled in your light. The largest leaps of faith can be accomplished with ease when I jump from fear to trust. And when I fall, you help me dust myself off and enter a new day cloaked in faith. I know now that my fragility is only weakness if I don't give it over to your transforming strength.

RESTORATION

Renewed to Love

Create in me a pure heart, O God,
and renew a steadfast spirit within me.
PSALM 51:10

Yesterday was a day of work, errands, making my way through traffic, and slogging through a maze of online ads and threads of conversation. It didn't make me feel shiny and new—or even productive. Instead, I went to bed restless and disappointed. Even this morning, I feel covered in residue, as though I'm unable to shed layers of the world's debris that I take on each day. I want to be a new creation.

Refresh me today, Lord. Renew in me a spirit that is faithful, diligent, and passionate about staying pure in the way I love others, set priorities, and express you. When the grime of earthly living covers me, help me to rise up and shake off the debris. Help me to protect the purity of my heart with all that I am and all that I do. It is with this heart that I can love my enemies, my family, and my neighbor with your love.

Resting on the Rock

Truly my soul finds rest in God...Truly
he is my rock and my salvation; he is
my fortress, I will never be shaken.

PSALM 62:1-2

Questions flood my mind with such force that I don't pause to listen for your answer. The pace of life is starting to lap me and my ability to take sure steps. You call me to stop and rest. You draw my spirit to stillness—not to squelch the questions, but to create space for the answers and to restore my faith.

When I'm ready for a next step, you encourage me to place my full weight on the rock of who you are. Here, I can safely take in the 360-degree view of my life with a clearer eye and mind. I find my bearings when protected in the fortress of your strength and my salvation. Suddenly, the questions don't have power to shake my foundation; instead, they offer reasons for me to seek your leading and rest in your will. Today, I will welcome the questions and joyfully look toward your answers.

Help Me to Be That Person

*A generous person will prosper; whoever
refreshes others will be refreshed.*

PROVERBS 11:25

Lord, I want to be the one who uplifts others with words of refreshment and gestures of kindness. Release me from any frugality of spirit. I don't want to be restricted in my giving by a heart that has learned its limits from those who have withheld love from me. After all, your love does not have strings attached; it has lifelines. Countless lifelines. That's the love I'm talking about. People are drawn to it because they hunger for your limitless refreshment.

Let me open the floodgates of generous love for my family and those around me today. Free me from the desire to demand results or reciprocation in order to keep on giving the refreshing, compassionate love of Jesus with an open heart.

Once More, with Feeling

*I will give you a new heart and put a new
spirit in you; I will remove from you your
heart of stone and give you a heart of flesh.*

EZEKIEL 36:26

God, I come to you with the hope of having my heart restored by your grace. When daily matters take over my every conversation, concern, and pursuit, I realize that I am not relating to life on a soul level. I become distant from you. Grant me the wisdom to switch gears from a matter-of-fact manner to a matters-of-the-heart intention. Help me make this transition so forgiveness, compassion, and understanding inspire my choices and shape my priorities.

Teach me to behold your children—*all* your children—with renewed mercy and sensitivity. Give me the vision and patience today to be a loving witness to another's life.

PEACE

What Do You See?

*I know, my God, that you test the heart
and are pleased with integrity.*

1 CHRONICLES 29:17

God, when you look at all that I am, what do you see? I begin each day hoping to live my time on this earth with a presence of peace and with integrity. This will only happen when I fully place my trust in you. I ask for discernment from you, Lord. I will be in your Word and draw from it the wisdom and principles you want all your children to grasp and live out.

Help me step back from my circumstances with patience so I can pray for right choices and actions. Forgive me when I become headstrong and strive for independence more than integrity. God, I pray that you see my willing heart and are pleased. I long to be a person of depth, humility, and honor, at peace with your ways.

When I Get in the Way

Submit to God and be at peace with him...Accept instruction from his mouth and lay up his words in your heart.

Job 22:21-22

How often has my strong will blocked me from submitting all of my life to your care? I'm working on this. I truly crave the peace that comes with surrender. I know it's an exchange of my fears and uncertainties for your truth. I get the better end of this deal, Lord. How gracious you are to me. Give me a willing heart that stores up your wisdom so it will fill me, overflow into my life, and become my first and only source of what I need and what I give to others.

When I get in my own way of this happening—and we both know this will occur—nudge my heart with your instruction. I want to clear the path so I can walk in your sweet ways.

PEACE

Looking for a Fight

Seek peace and pursue it.
PSALM 34:14

It is one of those mornings when everything I say is taken wrongly by others. I know a conversation is going a bad direction when I start interpreting the other person's sighs as offensive words. I've been here enough to know that within minutes this situation can snowball toward an unfortunate result. But it is hard to stop. I imagine the turn from bad to worse is my fault. Some days I just feel off and am looking for an outward battle to represent the one stirring in my spirit. Why doesn't my heart take a fast U-turn toward peace?

God, give me a desire for peace even as momentum gains within me to make my point. If my point or theory isn't about loving and honoring you, then I'm already off track. Thank you for letting me be vulnerable and never withholding your peace from this very human heart of mine.

My Peacekeeper

You will keep in perfect peace those whose
minds are steadfast, because they trust in you.

Isaiah 26:3

Everyone is winging it in this life unless they're partnering with you for each step, each hope. You've changed me from someone who befriended fear because it felt normal into one who is steadfast in trusting you. You are the protector of my heart, family, days, purity, wholeness, purpose, and faith. You are the peacekeeper who steadies my spirit with words of assurance and comfort.

Lord, you are my foundation and my dear shepherd. When I face unstable terrain, you remind me that I don't know what you know. This awareness fills me with deeper peace because I am with you, the one who *does* know. Thank you for all the roles you serve in my journey. My heart is bursting with gratitude.

REFRESHMENT

Refreshed by You

*Let my teaching fall like rain and my words
descend like dew, like showers on new grass,
like abundant rain on tender plants.*

DEUTERONOMY 32:2

Lord, cover me with your wisdom. Drench my dry mind with the dew of your words. I want to soak up your teaching so that I experience, from head to toe, the fullness of your truth. You didn't come to have a relationship with us so we would merely take notes and lock away your ideas of love and compassion. You came so we would have life and have it abundantly.

My skin and my limbs, my spirit and my cells—every part of me wants to be nourished by your sustaining manna. Turn my life from a parched organism into a living force that thrives and produces fruit. Help me encourage others to stand beneath the showers of your love.

How I Need You

*I will heal my people and will let them
enjoy abundant peace and security.*

JEREMIAH 33:6

God, for years I've spoken to others about your peace that passes all understanding. Now I realize that I didn't fully understand it until today. I know that I desperately need the healing power of your abiding, mysterious peace. I understand the fragility of my human condition more deeply. It's as if I've awakened from delusions of self-sufficiency, and there is no going back. I need you. I need your healing. I need the security of your promises.

How I love you, Lord. You want me to enjoy your abundant peace and experience it when questions arise, my relationships need mending, my body needs healing, and my thought patterns need rerouting. I am broken before you this morning, but I've never felt more whole.

Never Hungry

*You will have plenty to eat, until you are
full, and you will praise the name of the LORD
your God, who has worked wonders for you;
never again will my people be shamed.*

JOEL 2:26

have had lean years. I have faced times when there wasn't enough money to cover our needs—or so we thought. But you have always carried me through. My hunger is not physical, but spiritual. Lead me to the banquet of your Word, so I can dine on your nourishment until my soul is sated. All I need to do is sit at your table to be fed and filled. I know that the lean times of the spirit have happened only when I have forgotten about your invitation to join you and receive the feast of faith.

Forgive me, God, for the times when I forget about the wonders at your table. I praise your name. Today is a day to fill up. Never again will I need to be hungry. Let me never again turn away from your bounty.

Deeper Meaning

*In him you have been enriched in every way—
with all kinds of speech and with all knowledge.*
1 CORINTHIANS 1:5

I look back on the people who have had a positive influence in my life, and I know that they shared from the well of your knowledge. I want to be this kind of person to others. I realize that my depth of understanding comes from you. Help me to seek your thoughts and come to you for guidance each day so I'll be able to know and speak your truth to my family and those I encounter.

Shape me into a person who builds up others with words and ideas that are born of time spent in your presence. And as I learn to listen more closely to you, may I also become more compassionate, available for friends, family, and coworkers. I want all that pours forth from my heart and speech to come from the abundant source of your love.

SATISFACTION

Everything Tastes Better

*A person can do nothing better than to eat
and drink and find satisfaction in their own
toil. This too, I see, is from the hand of God, for
without him, who can eat or find enjoyment?*

ECCLESIASTES 2:24-25

ord, I experience renewal and reconnection with
you when I worship you. Whether it's upon waking, or after church, or after I have shared of your goodness during the day, these are times of gratitude. These
are moments when I pause to adore you and thank you
for what comes from your hand. There is joy when I
recognize the source of all that is good.

Life's joy can be found in the simplicity of faith. I
tend to complicate my pursuit of contentment because
I base the "achievement" of that joy on financial goals,
professional status milestones, or the completion of
house projects. How did I get so sidetracked by these
things? There's no reason to wait for the enjoyment of
this gift of life. I begin this day with all that I need.

Awakening to Satisfaction

*Satisfy us in the morning with your unfailing love,
that we may sing for joy and be glad all our days.*

PSALM 90:14

I opened my eyes this morning, Lord, and my gaze stayed on the view outside my window. I think of the birds who find the highest branch of a flowering shrub so they can take in the view and sing their songs—songs that sound like praise responses to all you have created. But me? I want to roll over and hit the snooze button. Everything about my life should lead me to do as the birds do…to sing with joy. What stops me? I love you, and I have so much to be grateful for.

Instead of turning over to get more sleep, I will turn over a new leaf to open up my gratitude. Satisfaction begins when I recognize you as Lord, as *my* Lord, and I welcome the day you have created for me. I am humbled, dear Creator. You do satisfy my soul.

Complete and Content

*I know what it is to be in need, and I know
what it is to have plenty. I have learned
the secret of being content in any and every
situation, whether well fed or hungry, whether
living in plenty or in want. I can do all
this through him who gives me strength.*

PHILIPPIANS 4:12-13

God, you always have the great ideas first! I've noticed there are more and more books, blogs, and songs about the importance of being happy with what we have, rather than dissatisfied about what we don't have. But you've been encouraging your children with this message through the words of Paul for ages. (Note to self: When I become discontent with any part of my life, I can seek renewed perspective through God's strength and Word.) I pray that I will never settle for the unease and ungrateful status of dissatisfaction. May I begin each day with a hunger for you so that I am made complete and content by your mending and very satisfying love.

The Peace of "Enough"

*Do not be anxious about anything, but in every
situation, by prayer and petition, with thanksgiving,
present your requests to God. And the peace of God,
which transcends all understanding, will guard
your hearts and your minds in Christ Jesus.*

PHILIPPIANS 4:6-7

No longer will "more" be my mission statement. A desperation comes over me when I doubt your provision or gauge my security based on what I have attained. Why do I feel compelled to add earthly measures of security to your divine care? The size of my house and bank account have nothing to do with my wholeness. When I anxiously dwell on the unknowns that lie ahead for me and my family, you call me back to the basics that matter. Everything else is a false fortress. I came into this world naked and crying, and you provided all I would need. Your plan for my life was set in motion, and so was the peace that remains my hope. I will walk through today knowing this, Lord, is enough.

FULFILLMENT

Hope for the Sweet Life

A longing fulfilled is sweet to the soul.
PROVERBS 13:19

God, I have watched you move in my life with a gentle force. There's no denying that you are the giver of all good things, including the hope I have to see possibilities unfold. In seasons of hardship, I cling to you. In seasons of amazement, I acknowledge your hand in all that happens. I am trying to set my mind on you each morning so that my thoughts are, in a way, grounded in heaven.

You know the longing I hold dear right now. I begin the practice of offering that longing up to you anytime I think of it. I lift it up to your care and ownership because, should you ever ask me to let go of it, I want to be willing. And should it be fulfilled, I want to praise your name with all that I am and with sweet words of gratitude.

Shape This Heart

*The LORD will vindicate me; your
love, LORD, endures forever—do not
abandon the works of your hands.*

PSALM 138:8

Jesus, shape me. Shape this heart and this life, Lord. Encourage my spirit so I can have hope that I am a creation in progress. I come to you on my knees today, and I let the hard words and emotions flow. I cry to you, Lord—please don't abandon the work of your love. I long to be filled and fulfilled by your purpose.

I have stretched and struggled, often in my own power. I am weary and wanting, and you are mighty and merciful. I want this day to be in your hands, where it can be formed to serve you. I pray for restoration in small and large ways. As each morning unfolds toward an evening…and each day unfolds toward the duration of a week, month, and year…let my life be a shining example of your unfailing, enduring love. And may I always give you praise for your mercy.

All of My Heart

*May he give you the desire of your heart
and make all your plans succeed.*

PSALM 20:4

I love to enter your presence. Here, my focus is on you, and I turn away from distractions—including my worries. Most people learn that others will eventually let them down. I'm no different. But I have a joy and a promise that fill my spirit with pure delight: You won't let me down. In fact, you remind me to call out for you and to seek you whenever I need to with the certainty that I will be answered.

When I face a hard day because someone is failing me or I am failing myself, you're right there to remind me of your plan for good that's unfolding in my life. Today, I give to you all of my heart so I can be sure the desires it holds are from you and are destined to be fulfilled by you for your divine purpose.

Let Me Be an Encourager

*Let us consider how we may spur one
another on toward love and good deeds.*

HEBREWS 10:24

I'm in awe of certain people who step up to do good in this world. I admire the convictions that shape leaders and become the catalyst for paths of change and hope. Lord, I want to cling to your hope and speak of it, so it will be a light to others.

You've given me the time to practice efforts of encouragement. My day and my life provide opportunities to live out this desire. May I lift up each person I meet today. Give me the right words that speak to each individual's heart, spurring them on to their best in you. Lord, when I set my sights on the grand picture of influence, retrain my vision on my home front first, and then on the expansive world you set before me.

RELIANCE

Today, I Dance

*You turned my wailing into dancing; you
removed my sackcloth and clothed me with joy,
that my heart may sing your praises and not be
silent. LORD my God, I will praise you forever.*

PSALM 30:11-12

like the view here, from the other side of a difficulty.
God, I can claim belief and lift praises after a long trial
because you have led me here in your grace. For a while
after my journey of strife, I was afraid to raise my voice
in victory. I was too immersed in doubt to do a happy
dance. That's what certain struggles do to me, Lord—
they make me fear that a glimmer of hope will be over-
shadowed by trouble once again. But you hold me in
your palm and tell me to trust. Trust and believe. So
today, I sing. I dance. And today, I will not be silent
about how you have guided me back to a place of hope.

You're It, God

*Since you are my rock and my fortress, for
the sake of your name lead and guide me.*

PSALM 31:3

I've set aside my how-to books, and I've turned down the volume of outside voices, Lord. I know that *you're* the one who should lead me in my life. I pray to feel your presence and guidance. Usher me in to deep trust. Give me a heart that can see, reach, and believe past my emotions and grab on to the great good in others and my circumstances.

You're the one I entrust my day to. This doesn't come easily, but I am committed to giving this day to you as an offering so that I can receive what you want for me in my spiritual journey. Let my first thoughts today come from your Word and your love so that my actions and choices will be inspired by your heart.

Holding Steady in Your Will

Teach me to do your will, for you are my God;
may your good Spirit lead me on level ground.

PSALM 143:10

had been plodding uphill for so long that I didn't notice at first how the terrain of my life has become level ground again. Now, I can catch my breath. I can sit quietly and ask for you to fill and refresh my spirit. I can call on you for this nourishment and infusion of faith whether I'm facing a tenuous incline or the momentum of a gentle slope.

Help me to draw strength from these times of walking level, solid ground with you. Guide me to listen more than I speak, appreciate more than I criticize, rest more than I resist, and enjoy this life more than I analyze it. Teach me how to have hope, not because circumstances are easy, but because every day is in your capable hands. I can hold steady in your will today with belief in possibility because I am held by you.

Out and About

*You wearied yourself by such going about, but
you would not say, "It is hopeless." You found
renewal of your strength, and so you did not faint.*

ISAIAH 57:10

Jesus, this is your stubborn child speaking. The
one who goes out and about at such a pace that
I become weary in all things and run in circles rather
than in the way you have for me. Now, I'm sensing
your big stop sign ahead on my path. I know it's time
to not merely have good intentions, but to be intentional in following your will for my life.

Take it easy. Draw strength. Center on your Word.
I believe you call me to these ways of hope and renewal.
You fill me up, Lord, and beckon me to deeper purpose,
rather than to farther distances. There is lovely rest for
the weary (that would be me) in the sanctuary of your
presence. Oh, Lord…let me seek your sanctuary today.

OPPORTUNITY

Responding in Kind

*As we have opportunity, let us do good
to all people, especially to those who
belong to the family of believers.*

GALATIANS 6:10

Soon after I called on you for grace, I turned around and was grumpy with someone who was trying to help me. I blamed them for my day, even though they were only trying to do their job. When will I learn to follow your lead and honor all people? God, help me seek joy. Better yet, help me be a creator of joy in all circumstances.

I see today as a chance to serve others and treat strangers and family with respect and kindness. I choose to see grumpiness, discomfort, or frustration as opportunities to put into practice the gift of grace.

Not of My Doing

*The race is not to the swift or the battle to
the strong, nor does food come to the wise or
wealth to the brilliant or favor to the learned;
but time and chance happen to them all.*

ECCLESIASTES 9:11

Oh, how I would love to claim responsibility for the opportunities I have either made or taken advantage of. This would give me a sense of great accomplishment and power. But, Lord, I know my good fortune is often the result of time and chance and your goodness. I am the recipient of your power when blessings shape my days.

When opportunity knocks, grant me the perspective and vision to see past my ego so I'll understand my role was merely to turn the knob, open the door, and welcome the opportunity. You made it, delivered it, and allowed me to recognize it. Thank you, Lord.

With God

Jesus looked at them and said, "With man this is impossible, but with God all things are possible."

MATTHEW 19:26

I love to feel in control. Self-reliant. Exuding a sense of independence is a must. At least, this is what I project to the world. Truthfully—and you already know this—I depend on you for everything. Just before that meeting, I was praying for the right words and the courage to face the unknown. Before I made a decision that would impact my family, I was on my knees seeking your will. I need and want to face every opportunity *with* you.

Lord, let me show others that you are my source of strength. Give me the confidence in you to stop keeping my weaknesses a secret. The more I reveal the truth, the better I will reflect the one who makes the weak strong and the impossible possible.

Create This Day

The pot he was shaping from the clay was marred in his hands; so the potter formed it into another pot, shaping it as seemed best to him.

JEREMIAH 18:4

Yesterday was a bit of a bust, Lord. My big plans withered, and my high hopes tumbled. My perfect, whole, flawless plan, once seen in the light of day, turned out to have cracks galore. So here I am, facing a new day and wanting it to be so much more. I have learned. I will give this day over to the potter's hands so that you can shape it.

I cannot wait to see what a day molded and prepared by you will look like. I bet it will be strong, beautiful, and whole.

PRODUCTIVITY

Seeing Your Purpose

Blessed are all who fear the LORD, who walk in obedience to him. You will eat the fruit of your labor; blessings and prosperity will be yours.

PSALM 128:1-2

I am in awe of you, Lord. And the more I understand your greatness and the extent of your power, the more willing I am to give my day over to you. Help me see that to walk in your way is the path to purpose and meaning. I want each day to count. Let the next 24 hours serve you, move me toward my personal best, and allow me to bear fruit that is pleasing to you.

Give me an understanding of productivity and purpose through your eyes, Lord. Then, when I face a detour or distraction, I will see it for what it is…a chance to turn around, follow your lead, and be fruitful.

Giving Myself Over

*Be diligent in these matters; give yourself wholly
to them, so that everyone may see your progress.*

1 Timothy 4:15

Giver of life, grant me passion and energy for all that I take on. Keep me bound to your Word so I am truthful and have integrity in all that I do. My schedule today includes difficult tasks…Help me be diligent and mindful in them so others will see the work of your hand. And when I face projects which seem mundane, let me see their worth.

God, I want to be a contributor. Strengthen me so I can give every moment my very best. In my times of reflection, meditation, and prayer, may I give 100 percent of my effort, as these are offerings to you, Lord.

Legacy of Peace

*LORD, you establish peace for us; all that we
have accomplished you have done for us.*

ISAIAH 26:12

Sometimes it takes chaos for me to better understand peace. When I am in the midst of circumstances that seem out of control or volatile, and I feel
a stillness deep within that allows me to still seek
you...I am sensing your peace. When rough times are
smoothed over and I am able to accomplish a goal, I
know I have witnessed the protection of your peace.

You do so much for me, Lord. Without you, I am
without direction. Without you, I could not achieve
anything of eternal value. Thank you, God, for caring
for your child.

Up to the Task

I consider my life worth nothing to me; my only aim is to finish the race and complete the task the Lord Jesus has given me—the task of testifying to the good news of God's grace.

ACTS 20:24

Is today the day I will learn to be an example of your grace, Lord? I hope so. I know that I have fallen short in the past. I start out with good intentions, but quickly drop them so I can reach for whatever suits me. Money. Success. Reputation. Status. These might reflect blessings from above, but they do little to share your grace with those around me.

If I want to look back upon my days with pleasure, I need to be productive as a servant, a helper, a caregiver, a friend, and a sharer of the gospel of your grace.

SERVICE

Full of Grace

Be wise in the way you act toward outsiders;
make the most of every opportunity. Let your
conversation be always full of grace, seasoned with
salt, so that you may know how to answer everyone.

COLOSSIANS 4:5-6

Open my ears to the needs of others, Lord. Let today be my chance to really hear what is being said by those around me. Often, my personal agenda fills my mind as others express their hearts. Grant me patience, openness, and compassion so I will be eager to understand another's need. Perhaps they will just need the listening, but maybe they will need comfort, or they might need to know of your goodness.

After listening, may I speak words that are of you and intended for that particular person. May I never let my own objectives override the conversation you intend.

Righteous Way

~

Do not repay anyone evil for evil. Be
careful to do what is right in the eyes of
everyone. If it is possible, as far as it depends
on you, live at peace with everyone.

Romans 12:17-18

Cover me, Lord…I'm going into my day. Protect me from my own desire to be right or to have my way. When I face someone who is not fair or just, give me the gift of silence or wise words to defuse the situation. I'll admit, sometimes I would rather prove someone wrong than prove peace is righteous.

Lead my mind to a peaceful solution. Give my heart the tenderness it needs to see beyond evil to the needs of the oppressed. And bless me, Lord, with the presence of mind to act in a righteous way that gives others a glimpse of you, the peacemaker of the soul.

Giving Out of Your Love

*If anyone forces you to go one mile, go
with them two miles. Give to the one who
asks you, and do not turn away from the
one who wants to borrow from you.*

MATTHEW 5:41-42

I cannot believe how much others expect of me. But today, I will face the demands of family, coworkers, and others who need my time with grace. When I answer my door, I know it will be for someone who wants something from me. Save me from my first reaction, which is to shut down...or shut that door. Allow me to go above and beyond what people are asking of me. You will give me the strength and ability to do so. I need not worry about my own shortcomings.

Today, I will come to you and ask for the patience, kindness, and love I need to go that extra mile.

Serving with My Gifts

Each of you should use whatever gift you have received to serve others, as faithful stewards of God's grace in its various forms.

1 PETER 4:10

I love gifts! I'm just not sure which ones I have, Lord. Give me your understanding of who I am in you. Allow me to see the gifts you have built into my heart and soul so that I can use this day for good. There are moments when I see my strengths in action, but I am not always consistent. Help me see the areas in my life that should be developed. Guide me to connect with anyone I can serve or comfort. Release me from insecurities that prevent me from sharing my gifts openly and wholeheartedly. Encourage me to let go of those activities or interests that are taking time away from what you would have me do. I want to get the most out of this life you have given me, Lord. I'm starting today with renewed vision and appreciation.

CHANGE

Like a Child

⌒

Truly I tell you, unless you change and become like little children, you will never enter the kingdom of heaven. Therefore, whoever takes the lowly position of this child is the greatest in the kingdom of heaven.

MATTHEW 18:3-4

How can I change my day today, Lord? In what ways do my grown-up thoughts keep me from embracing the pure, sincere faith of a child? Sometimes I think my goals hold me in a pattern of self-sufficiency, and I become unable to ask for help…even from you. My pride, my strong desire to find my own way as an adult, keeps me from bowing down at your feet and asking for your guidance and mercy.

Show me today how to give up control and accept the changes—both blessings and trials—that come with a humble, childlike faith.

Shape Me

*The Spirit of the LORD will come powerfully
upon you, and you will prophesy with them; and
you will be changed into a different person.*

1 SAMUEL 10:6

I give over my life to you this day. I submit my will to your will. By releasing my agenda into your hands, I will have the opportunity to see your power at work in my life. Where there is resistance, grant me peace so that I can let go. Where there is doubt, grant me understanding so that I might become wise. Where there is weakness, grant me wisdom so that I might defer to your strength.

God, each day I walk in faith should be a day I allow you to change me, shape me, and bring to fruition the potential you planted in me.

Let Me Be Consistent

*He who is the Glory of Israel does not lie
or change his mind; for he is not a human
being, that he should change his mind.*

1 Samuel 15:29

When I am not riding the fence with a decision, I am often wishing I had made another choice. My feet never seem to be on the firm ground of unwavering faith. I question everything and everyone because of my own faulty reasoning. God, help me focus on the path you have for me. Let my decisions be weighed against your Word and will…and then let me have peace as I move forward.

You are consistent, honest, and true. May the first decision I make every day be to follow your lead.

What Matters

*Command those who are rich in this present
world not to be arrogant nor to put their
hope in wealth, which is so uncertain, but to
put their hope in God, who richly provides
us with everything for our enjoyment.*

1 Timothy 6:17

Direct me to invest my time and energy today into matters of the heart. Steer me away from tagging value to temporal things of this world. You provide all that I need. When will I learn that my job is not to build an empire? My job is to serve in your kingdom. It seems I have spent a lot of my daydreams envisioning a life of ease, when my time would be better spent imagining how I might encourage others, aid the poor, and be sensitive to the wounded.

Remove my arrogance and replace it with a changed heart of humility. I will be watching for ways to place my hope in you.

DEVOTION

You Hear My Wailing

*Hezekiah turned his face to the wall and prayed to
the LORD, "Remember, LORD, how I have walked
before you faithfully and with wholehearted
devotion and have done what is good in your
eyes." And Hezekiah wept bitterly. Before Isaiah
had left the middle court, the word of the LORD
came to him: "Go back and tell Hezekiah, the
ruler of my people, 'This is what the LORD...says:
I have heard your prayer and seen your tears.'"*

2 KINGS 20:2-5

I pray that my life is worthy of your goodness through
your grace. I value my relationship with my creator
and long to walk faithfully beside you. I have felt deep
sorrow in my life, yet I have always known that you hear
my cries. I pray my desire to do right and live honorably
will be pleasing to you. When my trials cause me to have
doubts, may I also recall the times I cried out for help.

Remembering times of shared emotion inspires my
devotion.

Focusing on Truth

The works of his hands are faithful and just; all his precepts are trustworthy. They are established for ever and ever, enacted in faithfulness and uprightness.

PSALM 111:7-8

My thoughts pull me in many directions. When I turn to your precepts, your truths, I become focused and committed. Sometimes I pass through my days in a fog until I am confronted with a situation that needs attention and prayer. This is when I step out of my routine, my cruise-control mode, and step into my real life. I love this time when I feel your love, sense your guidance, and embrace your faithfulness.

I am the work of your hands. Forgive me when I forget this, Lord. Return me to situations that require the urgency of prayer and the desire to seek your truth.

Choosing Faith

*No one can serve two masters. Either you will
hate the one and love the other, or you will
be devoted to the one and despise the other.
You cannot serve both God and money.*

LUKE 16:13

As I rise and face my day, I notice that my thoughts often go to my financial needs. Not that I am planning major corporate takeovers...but I am dwelling on the daily ups and downs of my checking account. I feel the worry start to consume me until I can wrap my mind around a solution. I'm starting to realize how this misguided focus takes me away from serving the one I call my master.

Clear away this clutter, Lord. I want my waking thoughts to be devoted to you and your priorities for me. I give you complete control of my financial well-being. Let me feel the freedom of this choice.

Heart and Soul

*Devote your heart and soul
to seeking the LORD your God.*

1 CHRONICLES 22:19

From this moment on, I pray to give my heart and soul over to my caretaker. You made me. You know me. And you love me. I want to be a loyal follower who always seeks your face. When you shine your grace upon my day, my time becomes a brilliant offering of hope—not because of anything I have done, but because you give my ordinary life eternal value.

I wonder where I will find you during my day. The more I seek you, the more I will notice your hand on my life.

COMMITMENT

The Arc of a Promise

I establish my covenant with you: Never again
will all life be destroyed by the waters of a flood;
never again will there be a flood to destroy the earth.

GENESIS 9:11

Through the smear of water on my windshield today, I could just make out the road ahead. The wipers cut into my field of vision, and the rhythm of their motion lulled me into deep thoughts. Funny how moments like this bring me to questions about my life. Either I have concern about my day ahead, or I have unfounded worries tied to my unknown future.

But just as I pulled into a parking lot, I saw a brilliant rainbow framing the landscape beyond my reach. What a glorious reminder that you are committed to my day and the days that are out of my grasp!

As I thank you for the beauty of such colors against a dark sky, may I remember all the times you carried me from the floods of despair to the highlands of mercy.

Knowing Is Believing

Know therefore that the LORD your God is God;
he is the faithful God, keeping his covenant
of love to a thousand generations of those who
love him and keep his commandments.

DEUTERONOMY 7:9

You are God. You are the God of Adam and Eve. Your hands shaped the universe and every particle within its limitless mass. Every generation that has gone before has felt the presence of your power. I am following in the footsteps of people who have witnessed your love and care. Their stories remind me of your commitment to all your creation.

When I feel lost in the swirl of the cosmos, I can grab on to the certainty of this commitment. In turn, my daily commitment to you—to keep your commands—tethers me to the anchor of faith.

Words of Honor

All you need to say is simply "Yes" or "No";
anything beyond this comes from the evil one.

MATTHEW 5:37

Recently, I offered a half-hearted "yes" instead of sticking with my intended response of "no." Other times, I will decline the very thing I should be agreeing to. Help me make wise decisions, Lord. If my unwillingness to do something can be traced to laziness or lack of compassion, then lead me into a solid "yes." When a decision could distract me from the priorities you have for me, give my voice strength as I say "no."

I long to clearly discern the Spirit's leading. Make me sensitive to your calling on my life so that my answers and path can be straight and true.

I Give You This Day

Commit to the LORD whatever you do,
and he will establish your plans.

PROVERBS 16:3

Every moment that unfolds today is yours. I commit my thoughts, actions, reactions, and plans to you. I pray for your blessing upon my life, and I seek your strength when I face difficulties that might tempt me to falter in following your way.

When I begin to think this is just "any ol' day," give me a clearer sense of how great this day can be. My offerings, small and large, can be used by you to turn the next 24 hours into a great future.

HOPE

Finding Purpose in Hope

*May integrity and uprightness protect
me, because my hope, LORD, is in you.*

PSALM 25:21

With hope in my heart, I am stronger and lighter. A soul affected by hope is no longer bound to the weight of everyday transgressions. Hope gives wings to my dreams and inspires me to goodness. With your help, I can step up to a task with integrity and honesty. When the daily grind feels redundant, my hope in you helps me clearly see the purpose that is before me.

So much will be born out of hope today. May I recognize the gifts of security and faith and trust you to hold me up when nothing and no one else will.

Hope Endures the Wait

We wait in hope for the LORD;
he is our help and our shield.

PSALM 33:20

Today I will need help. No doubt about it. I seek you as my source of help and protection. Guide my steps, my words, my inclinations. I also have some burdens to give you. They are worries I have carried around for a while. But rather than wait for something bad to materialize from these frets, I will wait for your hope.

Knowing me, I will want to visit my worries from time to time. It is not easy to change my ways. Nevertheless, I trust in you, and I welcome hope into my life now that there is plenty of room.

Holding Fast

*Let us hold unswervingly to the hope we
profess, for he who promised is faithful.*

HEBREWS 10:23

I can never make up my mind when ordering from a
menu. Part of me wants everything listed. The other
part of me is scared that as soon as I make my choice, I
will realize it was the wrong one. God, don't let me be
this way with my profession of hope. Let my belief in
your promises be strong, decisive, and complete.

Life offers many choices. And with each one, there
is a risk. But my hope in you, Lord, is never a risk.

A Life of Hope

*Be joyful in hope, patient in affliction,
faithful in prayer. Share with the
Lord's people who are in need.*

ROMANS 12:12-13

This week, I would love to be a spokesperson for hope. Not in billboard and commercial kinds of ways…but in gentle, subtle ways. Let me translate the hope I receive through faith so others can discern it. Grace me with kind speech and a willing spirit.

When I can step away from my selfish concerns and see the needs of others, I will be able to fully embrace the intention of hope.

PROVISION

Turning First to You

I sought the LORD, and he answered me;
he delivered me from all my fears.

PSALM 34:4

When I seek you during my day, I will be reminded that you are the source of all I need. Instead of looking to others to make my way easier, I will seek your wisdom and strength. Instead of relying on my job to build me up, I will seek an identity grounded in you. Each time a need surfaces, let my thoughts go to my creator.

Today, I will encounter many opportunities to receive blessings and care from you. May I be mindful of each time your provision protects me, covers me, and nurtures me.

What Comes from You

~

The LORD said to Moses, "I have heard the grumbling of the Israelites. Tell them, 'At twilight you will eat meat, and in the morning you will be filled with bread. Then you will know that I am the LORD your God.'"

EXODUS 16:11-12

How many times have you met my cries for help with perfect provision? And how many of those times have I not even noticed? Lord, give me eyes to see what comes from your hand. My grumblings go on for so long that I have no voice left with which to praise you. And yet, you still extend mercy.

Turn my whining into rejoicing. May every gift I receive from you be an opportunity to tell others of your provision and forgiveness.

A Cause for Goodness

*Our people must learn to devote themselves
to doing what is good, in order to provide for
urgent needs and not live unproductive lives.*

Titus 3:14

I know that before the day is over, I will have labeled numerous things as "good." My morning latte, a conversation with a friend, a new recipe, a television show. But what will come from my lips, my hands, that is truly good in your eyes, Lord? Do my efforts provide what others need? I pray to have a day filled with goodness that affects people positively. I pray that my productivity moves me forward in your will.

Devotion is not a word used much these days. But I hope I can take on a spirit of devotion as I seek ways to honor the hope and purpose you give to me. Your every provision is good. May I share from this unlimited supply without hesitation.

Can I Have a Miracle?

*God gave Solomon wisdom and very great
insight, and a breadth of understanding as
measureless as the sand on the seashore.*

1 KINGS 4:29

I don't feel very wise today. Just the act of getting dressed and then heading out the door was draining…and now I am supposed to head into my day with purpose. God, expand my spirit, heart, and soul so that I can take in every bit of wisdom and understanding you give me. Stretch my sense of knowledge so I will have a heavenly perspective about what truly matters.

On days like this, when it seems to take a miracle for me simply to function, I pray for the provision of godly perspective. When I quit trying to be wise and learn to rest in your truth, I do believe life will open up in extraordinary ways. May this be the day I make that so.

PERSEVERANCE

Making It Through

*Do not throw away your confidence; it will
be richly rewarded. You need to persevere
so that when you have done the will of God,
you will receive what he has promised.*

HEBREWS 10:35-36

I f I can just get through this…" I find myself repeating
that statement often. I look for the silver lining that
will make a current task tolerable. My eyes scan the
horizon for the crossroads that will offer me an alter-
native to the burden of today. But perseverance is a
requirement of faith. I thank you for this part of the
journey, because I believe perseverance is also a gift.

When I do get through whatever is on my plate that
honors you, I know I will receive the promises you have
for me. If I do not know the sweat of the work, I will
never know the sweetness of the victory.

Love One Another

Keep on loving one another as brothers and sisters.

HEBREWS 13:1

Lord, help me. Today I will encounter a person who usually causes me to stumble. I get defensive in their presence. I'm not even myself when they enter the room. Why do I allow my emotions to get the best of me and turn a situation from good to bad? I am giving this situation over to you. And I am asking to see this person through your eyes rather than through my tainted lens of past experiences.

I feel good about this. I have never prepared for my interactions with this person through the power of prayer. Now, I will persevere in your strength and not my own...and that will change everything.

Gift of Compassion

As you know, we count as blessed those who have
perseverend. You have heard of Job's perseverance
and have seen what the Lord finally brought
about. The Lord is full of compassion and mercy.

JAMES 5:11

My mind goes to several friends today, Lord. They all are in need of your healing touch. Their journeys are filled with great difficulties. The darkness of fear covers their thoughts, even as they pray for hope. I pray that their perseverance leads them to see the blessings you will bring about. In their pain, you offer compassion and comfort. In their worry and uncertainty, you offer mercy.

I want to be a friend who encourages. Give me your words as I speak to them and lift them up in prayer.

Acceptance Speech

*When you sacrifice a thank offering to
the Lord, sacrifice it in such a way that
it will be accepted on your behalf.*

LEVITICUS 22:29

I want to thank you, God, for providing me with a life of meaning and opportunity. When I forgot how to move through my days, you encouraged me through the kindness of others, your Word, and glimpses of hope. Thank you for telling me the truth about your love. You shared your grace with my heart when I needed it most.

I wouldn't be where I am today if it weren't for you. There are many people to thank in my life, but I know the source of my understanding, belief, and inspiration is all you. Please accept my heartfelt thanks. I offer you my thoughts, my work, and my praises all day long.

CONTENTMENT

Open to Joy

*Create in me a pure heart, O God, and
renew a steadfast spirit within me...Restore
to me the joy of your salvation and grant
me a willing spirit, to sustain me.*

PSALM 51:10,12

Let my day be a clean slate that welcomes the hope and joy ahead, Lord. I no longer want to wake up to thoughts of losses, mistakes, or "should've" scenarios. As soon as I begin that tally, the day's potential joy is already lost.

"Restore to me the joy of your salvation." When I was buoyed by the release of my burdens to your care. I not only accepted joy, but watched for it to be a part of my experience. Time and circumstances have jaded that view. Remind me of the contentment of my faith.

Two Steps Forward...

Godliness with contentment is great gain.
For we brought nothing into the world, and we
can take nothing out of it. But if we have food
and clothing, we will be content with that.

1 Timothy 6:6-8

Why am I so quick to grab up things? Stuff consumes me. Fills my home. My thoughts. My space. I don't even *want* most of these things. Even with a discerning mind in this head of mine, I have given myself over to the marketing monster. I consider this foolish behavior, and beyond that, I consider the acquisition of things as irrelevant to a worthy life. God, remove this lust from my heart so that godly contentment will again be a part of my journey.

Pare away the trivial so that I might truly see what is of your hands. May I learn to recognize the resources you give me to use on this journey so that I might discover the life you intended for me.

What a Friend

You make known to me the path of life;
you will fill me with joy in your presence,
with eternal pleasures at your right hand.

PSALM 16:11

I am excited to think of spending time with a good friend today. We are able to talk about the real stuff of life and also give ourselves over to laughter that is true and deep, never self-conscious.

Lord, I know that in your presence, you offer a friendship even more vulnerable and joyful than this earthly one. I'm ashamed to say that I have forgotten this at times and have entered into your presence like a scolded child, rather than a person intending to experience the pleasures of being known and loved and cherished.

You carve out the path of my days through the history of time and experience. Help me step into the joy as well…and may I learn to rush into your presence with great expectations for contentment and lasting relationship.

Releasing My Restlessness

But the wisdom that comes from heaven is first of all pure; then peace-loving, considerate, submissive, full of mercy and good fruit, impartial and sincere.

JAMES 3:17

My restless spirit will not find peace until I come to you and ask you to take all of my life and shape it into being. You formed me in my mother's womb, yet I still hold tightly to what I claim to be "mine," including victories and worries. This does not allow me peace. Give me a glimpse today of what it means to give myself over to your wisdom fully. Walk me through this important lesson so I will release my grip.

Prosperity, trials, and the storms of life will be manageable and even welcomed when I know they, too, are under your sovereign rule in my life. No longer will such changes and circumstances cause my spirit to be anxious and uncertain.

Now

The Covering of a Life

If that is how God clothes the grass of the field, which is here today and tomorrow is thrown into the fire, will he not much more clothe you—you of little faith?

MATTHEW 6:30

As I get dressed today, I know that I am really facing the day naked and dependent upon you to clothe me. Your grace clothes me with forgiveness. Your mercy dresses me in compassion. Your love covers me with value. Every decision I make during my day relies on your guiding hand.

My faith has been small in many ways. But that was in the past. I want to outgrow that old faith so I can be dressed in the faith you have for me now.

One Thing at a Time

*Do not worry about tomorrow,
for tomorrow will worry about itself.
Each day has enough trouble of its own.*

MATTHEW 6:34

Slow me down, God. I use my energy each morning troubleshooting for the days ahead. I completely bypass the gift of today…the gift of now. Calm my spirit, expand my breaths, and fill me with your peace so that my spinning thoughts settle. I serve no greater good by thinking ahead, wringing my hands and wondering what might happen.

Save me from my need to control every possible situation. Lead me back to trusting you with all that will happen. I know that you do not ask me to handle everything on my own. You will be there with me…for me. So today, this moment is only about this moment. May I rest in it and experience it as you intended.

Seeking the Words

Whenever you are arrested and brought to trial, do not worry beforehand about what to say. Just say whatever is given you at the time, for it is not you speaking, but the Holy Spirit.

MARK 13:11

Give me the words I need, Lord. I have fretted over today's situation for some time now, and I realize how useless that worrying was. Just as you provide my daily bread, you will also provide the words and thoughts I need when pressures exist. Remove the spirit of fear that sweeps over me. Allow me to listen to the Holy Spirit for my leading.

I can rework phrases in my head now and hope it all turns out later. Or I can keep my thoughts on you and know you will take care of me when the time comes.

Following Your Lead

*Love the LORD your God with all your
heart and with all your soul and with all
your strength. These commandments that I
give you today are to be on your hearts.*

DEUTERONOMY 6:5-6

God, I want to use my many moments today to love you completely. When I catch myself wandering in thought, I will begin to praise you. When my day lacks energy, I will pray for your love to act through me. Fill my soul with understanding of you and your ways so that my "now" is infused with your presence.

Carve on my heart all that you hope for my life, Lord. I will follow this map each step of the way.

RENEWAL

Finding You

*If someone dies, will they live again? All the days
of my hard service I will wait for my renewal to
come. You will call and I will answer you; you
will long for the creature your hands have made.*

JOB 14:14-15

Whatever trouble today brings, I know the situation will be restored in your time. I have great relief knowing that my hard times will be shaped into good things. All I need to do is remember my life before I met you, and I understand what a new life is all about. Grace. Second chances. Renewal.

I long for you. The pace of my day might cause me to forget this…but in the quiet moments between sleep and wakefulness, I feel the pull toward your presence. And my joy deepens when I realize you long for me as well.

Shine

*Restore us, LORD God Almighty; make your
face shine on us, that we may be saved.*

PSALM 80:19

Some days are just colder than others. I need to feel
the warmth of your face shining upon me, Lord.
I want to be covered by your radiance. Resting in the
palm of your hand, I feel secure and saved. Lead me
back to this place.

Your promises will unfold as the day progresses.
And I will gather them close even as I am uncertain
about how the day will play out, because through your
promises comes renewal and wholeness.

Resurrection's Power

*We were therefore buried with him through
baptism into death in order that, just as Christ
was raised from the dead through the glory
of the Father, we too may live a new life.*

ROMANS 6:4

My personal resurrection in this life seems to be taking place slowly. I know that you gave me a new life when I gave my heart to you. But Lord, sometimes I fall back into old ways. I want the renewal given to me by grace through *your* resurrection. I want to see, taste, and feel what it means to live as a freshly conceived creation.

You carry me through the pain of death to the glories of life…yet some days, like today, I do very little to follow you wholeheartedly. Your love surprises me. Just when I feel hopeless, you give me a sign of renewal. An idea. A song. A prayer. A friend. Hope. These ordinary gifts remind me of your power to turn my weary heart toward wonder.

The Next New Thing

*You were taught, with regard to your former
way of life, to put off your old self, which is
being corrupted by its deceitful desires; to
be made new in the attitude of your minds;
and to put on the new self, created to be like
God in true righteousness and holiness.*

EPHESIANS 4:22-24

People talk about new attitudes. New ways of thinking. New ways of being. I tried that in the past, and
it was very difficult to maintain whatever new thing I
was trying to incorporate into my life. I wanted others
to identify me with this new choice, yet I wouldn't try
it out long enough for this to happen.

It is only when renewing of my mind and spirit
occurs that a transformation takes place in my life. My
earlier changes were surface level. Only this choice I
make to be yours will result in a change worth noticing.

TRIALS

When Trouble Comes

*If any of you lacks wisdom, you should ask
God, who gives generously to all without
finding fault, and it will be given to you. But
when you ask, you must believe and not doubt,
because the one who doubts is like a wave
of the sea, blown and tossed by the wind.*

JAMES 1:5-6

I find myself in a bit of a predicament—as you already know. This morning finds me facing some drama in my life. I have nobody to blame except myself. I denied your wisdom, even though you offered it to me. I turned my back on the leading of the Spirit. This all sounds negative…but in truth, this situation has led me back to you. Every time I forget who is really in control, I end up playing a role in some silly dilemma that could have been avoided.

I would say, "Never again," but I have said that before. For now, I will simply thank you for giving me the resources to work my way through this trial. And may I turn to you sooner, rather than later, next time.

Tuning In to You

*I urge you, brothers and sisters, by our Lord
Jesus Christ and by the love of the Spirit, to join
me in my struggle by praying to God for me.*

ROMANS 15:30

A tug on my heart this morning leads me to pray for my friends who are going through difficulties. I tuck them in my mind to remember throughout the day…but you know how busy life becomes. Starting off my day by lifting up others in prayer tunes my heart to be prayerful and mindful of these people, even when busy.

Grant me a prayerful nature. It takes work for me to practice this discipline, Lord, yet it also offers me a closeness with you that I long for. I draw near to you right now and pray for myself and others, that our trials will always lead us back to you.

Life Work Ahead

No discipline seems pleasant at the time, but painful. Later on, however, it produces a harvest of righteousness and peace for those who have been trained by it.

HEBREWS 12:11

How much work is required of me? Some days, I think I am stuck on a treadmill, rather than a road that leads somewhere. What do you ask of me, God? I know that most often I am running to follow the commands that come from others, myself, and the world around me...and not from you.

Help me see that the good work I do will have a harvest of righteousness. And let me identify the work I am racing to complete that serves no purpose other than feeding my ego. Give me the strength to choose that which serves you.

Spiritual Student

Come to me, all you who are weary and burdened,
and I will give you rest. Take my yoke upon you
and learn from me, for I am gentle and humble
in heart, and you will find rest for your souls.
For my yoke is easy and my burden is light.

MATTHEW 11:28-30

If I can look at my current trial as a form of education, I can almost deal with all that it is costing me: time, energy, heartache, headaches. But this also means that I need to follow the way of my teacher—and you are my teacher for life. All that I need to know and learn comes from my source of life and grace.

Bring me into your classroom every morning. When I sit at the back of the class, awaken my spirit and call on me, Lord. I am a pupil who needs to see what the master has for me. You do not give me problems for the sake of entertainment. You allow these problems so that I will come to you and ask for rest, guidance, and a lesson in faith.

PROMISES

Trust Takes Trials

*You know with all your heart and soul
that not one of all the good promises the
LORD your God gave you has failed.*

JOSHUA 23:14

It is easy to forget all you have brought me through. Not because I am not grateful, but because after a fall, I am always quick to embrace life and goodness. I don't want to look back or dwell on the troubles I have experienced. But I am realizing how important it is to remember these times. They strengthen my journey.

Today I begin a new kind of trial. I have never been here before—not exactly. But all I need to do is recall the promises you have planted in my spirit, and I trust you once again. The good news is that even if the trials are not getting easier, the trusting is.

Resting in the Unknowing

*As you do not know the path of the wind,
or how the body is formed in a mother's
womb, so you cannot understand the
work of God, the Maker of all things.*

ECCLESIASTES 11:5

I am clueless as to how today will turn out. Why do I even bother to guess, assume, or presume anything? I'm so ridiculous that way, wanting to feign that I am in control because times are hard. But I cannot know the big picture. I can only know that you are the one I should trust. I have many examples of your goodness and faithfulness in my life. I cling to these.

When people ask me what I am going to do or even why this is happening…I no longer want to fabricate my future actions or make up reasons. I want to rest in the unknowing. I want to rest in the security of my maker's plan and promises. Come what may.

The Power of a Plan

*"I know the plans I have for you," declares the
LORD, "plans to prosper you and not to harm
you, plans to give you hope and a future."*

JEREMIAH 29:11

struggle to accept that this really is the way to go. Personally, I wouldn't have done things this way...but you are God, and I am so very human. My vision is limited and failing. I tend to hold on to people or things that are meant to be released. And I second-guess everything. I'm not telling you anything you don't already know...

You also know that today I woke up and felt excited about the plan you have for me. I have finally given myself over to the idea of the future being about hope and not fear. It's a new thing for me...but I think I could get used to it.

Take This Day

I will sacrifice a freewill offering to you;
I will praise your name, LORD, for it is good.

PSALM 54:6

I pray to make this day a freewill offering to you. As I rise and begin my morning, may I consider the blessings around me so I will give you praise. May I think about the people I will interact with so that my heart will be prayerful. May I give decisions over to you so I stay within your will and move toward your purpose for me. May I observe the needs of others so I can serve them as your hands.

God, this day is yours. I give it freely so that I might know you and your ways better.

Awareness

Learning to Be Aware

Know also that wisdom is like honey for you:
If you find it, there is a future hope for you,
and your hope will not be cut off.

PROVERBS 24:14

Lately, I have moved through my days in a bit of a fog. I look back on the past week —the past month, even—and sense that I have not been aware of you and the lessons you would have me learn. I don't want to be someone who mentally checks out of their life. Even when I face difficulties, I will glean wisdom that feeds my soul.

Make me aware of what you would have me learn today, Lord.

In the Wake of a Day

Hear, Israel, and be careful to obey so that it may go well with you and that you may increase greatly in a land flowing with milk and honey, just as the LORD, the God of your ancestors, promised you.

DEUTERONOMY 6:3

This morning, I turned off my alarm, sat on the edge of the bed, and just listened to you. Before the flood of plans, thoughts, regrets, or schedule changes filled the space between my ears, I used my ears to take in your directions.

I pray to be aware of what you ask of me so that I can obey faithfully. I want to walk in your ways so that I can step into your promises.

Me Me Me

*Hear and pay attention, do not be
arrogant, for the LORD has spoken.*

JEREMIAH 13:15

I never thought my pride could actually block me from understanding you. But these days, I am stubborn... always trying to figure out the way on my own. I speak up on behalf of myself, my opinions, and my ego more often than I speak up for my faith. I let my concerns consume me before I turn to you in prayer.

So much *me* and so little *you* makes for a difficult life. I miss your gentle leading. My mind and heart are too scattered to take in your truths. I don't even taste your simple joys because I deem them insignificant. Help me strip away my own agenda and prideful ways so I have nothing blocking my view of you and your path.

Taking Notice

He returned to his disciples and found them sleeping. "Couldn't you men keep watch with me for one hour?" he asked Peter. "Watch and pray so that you will not fall into temptation. The spirit is willing, but the flesh is weak."

MATTHEW 26:40-41

Will you catch me sleeping today instead of being alert? How many chances do I miss to do right… to do good or to serve another? Please open my eyes to those I meet who need help that I can offer. Sharpen my mind so I can be discerning.

When I am tired, it is easy for me to fall back into old, bad habits. Grant me the energy to be careful and wise. When the wisdom I need is beyond my capacity, give me your wisdom to see the way through a situation.

COURAGE

Carry Me

*Let the morning bring me word of your unfailing
love, for I have put my trust in you. Show me
the way I should go, for to you I entrust my life.*

PSALM 143:8

feel like such a child. Today gives me too much worry
and grief and stress. I thought I could do it—carry
out the day—but I cannot. I need you, God. I not only
need you to be with me, but I need you to carry me
through this day. I started out so strong, but now that I
face the reality of moving forward, I cannot go it alone.

Show me the way. I lift up my day to you and pray
for courage to keep going. I trust you. And where there
is still resistance within me to rely on you instead of
myself, please remind me of this feeling in the pit of my
stomach and why I need you. You are my only source
of strength.

Needing a Savior

Those who know your name trust in you, for you,
LORD, have never forsaken those who seek you.

PSALM 9:10

I come into your presence today with a sheepish look and a heavy heart. I have been here before…countless times…and you have not forsaken me. But I feel so needy that sometimes I second-guess returning to you. Yet I know your name, and you are my holy redeemer. You are my Savior and Messiah. It is grace that falls from your lips, not a gavel of conviction when I am humble and in need.

God, grant me the peace that comes with your strength and courage. Do not let me turn my back on you when I so desperately require your guidance.

Returning to the Boat

Immediately he spoke to them and said, "Take courage! It is I. Don't be afraid." Then he climbed into the boat with them, and the wind died down.

MARK 6:50-51

Do I even recognize you when you enter my boat to calm the storms and save my soul? Have I ever looked past you as I watch for a savior that seems bigger, stronger, and more able to pull me from the clutches of the waves? I know I have…because my self-doubt can make my faith weak. Yet you are faithful each time, and my worries fade.

I do take courage in you. I will not look beyond your shoulders to the night sky in search of more. I will trust, because you are the one who returns to the boat of my life and tells me not to be afraid.

Leaving It All Behind

Peter answered him, "We have left everything to follow you! What then will there be for us?"

I look around me and notice the absence of some things. While some luxuries or opportunities have been excluded from my world out of preference, some have been sacrificed so that I could live a life to better serve you and those I love. I am so thankful I came to know you and the gift of your grace. At that time, many unnecessary trappings and circumstances fell away. Now I face each day hoping that I have pared down my life to the bare essentials.

God, you do not leave me wanting for anything. So please give me the courage and insight to leave behind all that I do not need in my life for your glory's sake.

THIRST

The Hunger of the Void

*Blessed are those who hunger and thirst
for righteousness, for they will be filled.*

MATTHEW 5:6

Sometimes I can skate over the voids in my life. I don't even look down to see if the chasm still exists because I don't want to know. But on days like today, I cannot get up without asking for you to fill that void. I know it is there, and I know I cannot skate, skip, or jump over it…even in a state of denial. The hunger comes from deep within, and it does not fade when I puff up my own ego or worth.

My hunger and thirst lead me back to your righteousness, Lord. Only you can fill this place that questions, missteps, and becomes empty when ignored. Fill this place in me and let it overflow to all that I do and am.

Seeing the Answer

*He humbled you, causing you to hunger and
then feeding you with manna, which neither you
nor your ancestors had known, to teach you that
man does not live on bread alone but on every
word that comes from the mouth of the LORD.*

DEUTERONOMY 8:3

When I ask you for wealth, what is it you send instead? When I ask for bread, what nourishment do you bestow upon me and my family? When I lack, what is it you give to me to make up for my weakness? All that carries me into my life and through it comes from your hand and the sustenance you provide.

When my stomach growls, I may question what I see falling from heaven to fill my plate. But Lord… I receive these gifts with faith, believing that you are guiding my journey and you do not leave your children to starve.

Beyond Reasons

*I was hungry and you gave me something to
eat, I was thirsty and you gave me something
to drink, I was a stranger and you invited
me in, I needed clothes and you clothed
me, I was sick and you looked after me, I
was in prison and you came to visit me.*

MATTHEW 25:35-36

The needs of my brothers and sisters around me are so great that I do not know where to start. There is a strong desire, a thirst to quench, to reach out and help others. But then I sit back and list the stipulations or the reasons this could go very wrong. This is when I think of you telling us to feed, clothe, and aid the sick and visit the imprisoned, and it is clear you do not ask me to question...you ask me to serve.

May I truly see you in those I will help today. And when I cannot, give me the strength to continue giving. Because even when I am blind to you, you are the one who stands before me asking for more.

153

Learning to Knock

*Ask and it will be given to you; seek and
you will find; knock and the door will
be opened to you. For everyone who asks
receives; the one who seeks finds; and to the
one who knocks, the door will be opened.*

<small>MATTHEW 7:7-8</small>

Maybe I lived through too many fundraisers as a kid to feel comfortable enough to stand in front of a door and knock. I think about the possible rejection and ignore the desire within me to know the one on the other side. I consider other ways I could go about asking for assistance—a phone call, a letter, an email—and they seem so much better suited to my personality.

Lord, get my clenched fingers to start knocking. The excuses rush over my good intentions like a tidal wave. Yet I understand that you require me to come to you, humbled, seeking, and thirsty. This is when you answer the door. But first…I must knock.

TRANSFORMATION

Open and Unfolding

*To all who did receive him, to those
who believed in his name, he gave the
right to become children of God.*

JOHN 1:12

Jesus, today I want to be in your presence as your child. Tell me stories about your love and about who I am in you. I sense your hand on my head as you comfort me. And you nudge me with encouraging words when I try new things. When I'm open to transformation, you remind me to allow joy and renewal to surprise me and change me. I imagine the concern in your eyes when you realize I'm holding on to a past hurt even after you've shown me how you healed that wound. I no longer want to tend to something old and lifeless just because it is oddly comforting to return to former pain.

Lord, give me ears to hear and a spirit to receive your story about my future and ongoing transformation. This is a new day and an unfolding chance to believe fully in you.

New Life

The perishable must clothe itself with the
imperishable, and the mortal with immortality.

1 CORINTHIANS 15:53

God, I'm turning my heart toward all that is eternal. I will take inventory of my life and proceed to clean house spiritually and otherwise. Maybe I'm motivated by the sun that sheds light on the dusty places of my days. Or perhaps I've grown tired of being stuck, staid, and discontent in the musty old ways of being. Whatever the reason, I have a strong desire to offer up to you all that is dead and dying in my life: worn habits, tired words, broken promises, deflated dreams, and the sins of indifference and apathy. I know that change will not be easy, but I'm ready for your breath of life to usher me and my family toward hope, actions, words, beliefs, and everlasting love.

Turned into Praise

He put a new song in my mouth,
a hymn of praise to our God.

PSALM 40:3

I rise today with the hope of goodness and joy ahead. I'm shedding the mind-set that my life is ordinary, going nowhere specific, or merely a practice of using up time. This isn't the way you want me to think of the gift of life you've given me. Take all that I am, Lord, and shape me into the creation you designed me to be. Let my sacred journey as a child of God be an example of all-out faith.

The words from my lips might seem to be about everyday matters, but I know that you're giving me a new song. This song will take regular moments and conversations and transform them into opportunities to praise you. There is nothing ordinary about that.

Stay

*Brothers and sisters, each person, as responsible
to God, should remain in the situation
they were in when God called them.*

1 Corinthians 7:24

Surely you jest. This is what I am thinking sometimes as I head into the situation you have placed me in lately. This couldn't possibly be of God, of your hand. Could it? Lord, give me perspective on this. Maybe I just want to avoid this kind of responsibility. It seems there is rarely a break from it. Maybe there are lessons you want me to learn right now.

I will remain here because you remain beside me. I couldn't do this alone. Please help me see inklings of the purpose for this time and place in my life. When I do not see the reason, please give me the inspiration. Transform my perspective so that I stand here with confidence and stay in your presence with hope.

DIRECTION

Show Me Your Will

*Be very careful, then, how you live—not as unwise
but as wise, making the most of every opportunity,
because the days are evil. Therefore do not be
foolish, but understand what the Lord's will is.*

EPHESIANS 5:15-17

Discerning your will is hard. I start my day asking
for your guidance so that I will make good decisions and follow the path you want me to take. But
by lunchtime, I often lose any sense of an inner tug. I
will rely on my knowledge of your Word, and that will
carry me through the situations, conversations, and
choices I face. But today, I just want to know if I am
close to being right in your will.

Please direct me and my thoughts so I can look at
my life through your eyes and your heart. I long to walk
with you all of my days.

Shape My Steps

*In their hearts humans plan their course,
but the LORD establishes their steps.*

PROVERBS 16:9

I have big plans for my day. I will be productive, creative, and efficient…and graceful as I accomplish so much. Okay, maybe my real plan is just to survive. But faith stretches my motives toward bigger purposes. I see how even the smallest acts can be turned into blessings. I realize my accidental moments might be part of your intentional plans.

I just have to be facing the right direction…toward you.

The Release of Compassion

Consider the blameless, observe the upright;
a future awaits those who seek peace.

PSALM 37:37

Sometimes my direction comes from within. Not only from your guiding presence, but from a driving force you've placed in me. I'm still looking for my personal passion. But lately, I have felt led by the power of peace. My heart is tenderer. Compassion comes more easily.

Where will this newfound sensitivity take me? How do you want it to impact my life and the lives of those around me? Show me how to allow more peace into my days, and I will take that wisdom with me into my future.

Purify My Heart

There is surely a future hope for you, and your
hope will not be cut off. Listen, my son, and
be wise, and set your heart on the right path.

PROVERBS 23:18-19

Keep my path straight. I become easily distracted, but I want to stay on track. I pray that you will bring people into my life who will guide me when I do step off the intended route or become fascinated by the wrong map. Nudge me with ideas and things I read. Fill my mind with whatever it takes to steer me toward wisdom.

My prayer today is for purity. Save me from the clutter and mess that taints my viewpoint. I want to be free and willing to embrace the hope of my future.

AUTHENTICITY

Sharing the Real Me

*The LORD detests lying lips, but he delights
in people who are trustworthy. The prudent
keep their knowledge to themselves, but
a fool's heart blurts out folly.*

PROVERBS 12:22-23

Oh Lord, help me be truthful today. No more gossip or little white lies. No more hedging my answers to pacify people or sway arguments. I want to be authentic in my speech, thoughts, and actions toward others. Can I admit that I don't always know myself? I can confuse who I think I ought to be with who I really am.

But Lord, you know me better than I do. Please reveal to me the ways that are authentic for me. Lead me toward your truths so I can rest in them and use them as my foundation.

Good, Right Intentions

*As servants of God we commend ourselves in every
way: in great endurance; in troubles, hardships
and distresses; in beatings, imprisonments
and riots; in hard work, sleepless nights and
hunger; in purity, understanding, patience and
kindness; in the Holy Spirit and in sincere love;
in truthful speech and in the power of God.*

2 Corinthians 6:4-7

Protect my role as a believer, Lord. Guard my reputation and my actions. Give me a cautious spirit so that I wait before I speak out. Preserve my intentions so that they are pure and righteous. Direct me toward the ministry which suits my gifts so I serve you well with unfailing devotion.

I long to be sincere as I serve you, and others, in your power.

May I Be Faithful

*It is required that those who have been
given a trust must prove faithful.*

1 CORINTHIANS 4:2

When today is over, I hope you will have found me to be a true servant. May my actions have been pleasing to you and worthwhile to your children. I pray you will find my heart to be right and faithful in the work I have done. My day is an offering to you that cannot be repeated. Only today will I have this particular set of circumstances. What I do with these opportunities is a reflection of my belief in you.

Lord, I hope to do what is required of me…and to go even beyond this. At the end of this day, I hope to be a blessing to my creator.

Motivated by Love

I am not writing you a new command but one we have had from the beginning. I ask that we love one another. And this is love: that we walk in obedience to his commands. As you have heard from the beginning, his command is that you walk in love.

2 John 5-6

From the beginning of the day until the passing of the night beneath the stars, I pray that I follow the command born of your will: to love one another. Give me your heart for others so that my thoughts turn to compassion and unity rather than judgment and separation.

I pray for this day and all those to come…each one an opportunity to show you to the world and to show you my faithfulness. It is out of gratitude that I step into my morning. It is with humility that I turn to you throughout the day. Lead me with love so that I may follow in the path of love forever.

About the Author

Hope Lyda is an author whose devotionals, novels, and prayer books, including the popular *One-Minute Prayers® for Women* and *Life as a Prayer*, have sold more than one million copies. Her inspirational books reflect her desire to embrace and deepen faith while journeying to God's mystery and wonder.

Hope has worked in publishing for more than 20 years, writing and coming alongside other writers to help them shape their heart messages. As a trained spiritual director, she loves to help others enter God's presence and pay attention to their authentic, unique life and purpose. Her greatest joy is to find ways to extend these invitations through the written word and writing exercises.

She and her husband, Marc, have been married for more than 25 years and live in Oregon.

Contact Hope at hopelyda@gmail.com

Learn more at www.hopelyda.com

Follow on Instagram @hopelydawrites

MORE FAVORITE READS
FROM HOPE LYDA

Life as a Prayer
One Minute with Jesus for Women
One-Minute Prayers® for Wives
One-Minute Prayers® for Moms
One-Minute Prayers® for Women

AVAILABLE AS E-BOOKS
One-Minute Prayers® for Young Women
Hip to Be Square (fiction)
Altar Call (fiction)
Life, Libby, and the Pursuit of Happiness (fiction)

To learn more about Harvest House books and
to read sample chapters, visit our website:

www.harvesthousepublishers.com

HARVEST HOUSE PUBLISHERS
EUGENE, OREGON